Inside
OF YOU

CHERISE BURRELL

CHOOSE2CHANGE
PUBLISHING

Published by Choose 2 Change Publishing

www.c2cpublishing.com

ISBN: 979-8218076283

First Printing, September 2022

10 9 8 7 6 5 4 3 2 1

Dedication

To my late grandmother Susie Mea Burrell

*whom I never had the pleasure to meet but your love
and legacy lives on*

Acknowledgements

I would like to acknowledge my mother Lillian Edmond who I love dearly! Thank you for the many days and nights, you wore the hat of being our mother and father, making sure we were well taken care of.

To my father who lost his mother at a young age and struggled in life. I never understood your life until you passed. I understand your pain now and it helped me to realize you gave all that you had to give to me, and I truly wished I could tell you; I forgive you and I've learned your love for me was not in vain!

My oldest granddaughter Kendall Cherise Ward who questioned me weekly about my book until I finally told her I was done.

My children Ray-Ray, Virgil and Ebony who inspired me to want more out of life and influenced me to push for higher levels.

Dr. Wayne Dyer and Oprah Winfrey who I would listen to and or watch on YouTube!

A host of family and friends who are excited about my writing and coaching!

Table of Contents

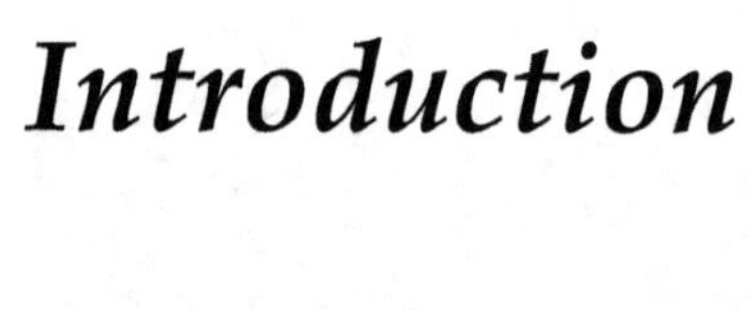

Introduction

Introduction

Everyone has a story about their life. Everyone has shared in good and bad experiences. You are not alone, your story is important, although every story has its own uniqueness, there's always someone out there who's story may mirror yours.

We all have experienced some level of pain, joy, loneliness, disappointment etc. There are certain places, people, and situations that have turned our lives upside down, bringing an intense amount of pain, trauma, and sorrow. As we continue to travel through life, the heavy weight of the pain and or trauma begins to affect us in almost every area of our lives. To alleviate some of the weight, we must heal. We must look inside ourselves and heal from the inside out.

Let's focus on that word for a minute, say it again "heal"! What does healing mean? What impact does it really have? How do we do it or how does it happen? I have answered those questions for you within the next few chapters of this book.

I knew one day I would be writing a book, but I thought it would be more about what I've been through. My past hurts were horrible and humiliating, thank God that is not what he wants me to put in this book, but God allowed me to go through to grow through.

Today, I'm healed throughout, and I understand the pain was a tool used to bring forth healing. Thank God for the pain, without it we would be a mess, it teaches one to be humble, fight, want, desire, and mostly to overcome. I never thought I would be writing about healing I really didn't see this coming, but I'm excited to walk alongside you as you begin your healing journey or as you continue to heal, let your healing transform the trajectory of your life.

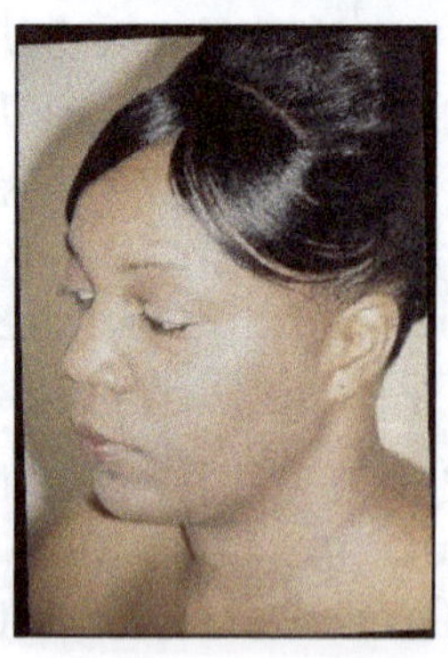

Part I

The Beginning of Trauma

Chapter One

Time of Conception

February 5th, 1968

Mrs. Lillian Burrell and Mr. Leon Burrell had a divine appointment to conceive who they would one day call Cherise Burrell.

A baby girl who will be the manifestation of their appointment. I wish I knew the time of day or the emotional condition they were both in at that moment. However, listening to what would later be a separation I can't help but to believe there was already a brewing detachment.

Was my parents' relationship and environment healthy? Well, I don't know for sure, but what I do know is I have siblings outside of my mom's children that are very close in age, so that revealed to me that my mother was not happy. They were married with three small children and about to give birth to their fourth child. When my mother went into labor with me, she was home alone with the children. She called my aunt and uncle to help her get to the hospital and to keep an eye on the other children.

Mom describes this moment as very depressing and mentally exhausting. Her exhaustion wouldn't provide her the strength to push, so she says I delivered myself as she laid there having what we may call today a "mental meltdown". When the nurse tried to hand me to my mother, she declined, she was too tired.

I was born October 28th, 1968, in the early morning to an overly strained but loving mother and an alcoholic father. I came in weighing 9 pounds, 11 ounces. I recall my mother sharing with me that I practically walked into the world. One of my uncle's visited the hospital, he was the first family member to hold me and at that moment he described me as a butterball turkey.

My father however, never made it to the hospital, and this is how I would start the rest of my journey here on Earth. I asked my mother "When was the first time my dad saw me?", she couldn't recall our first meeting. My father was in his own world and at that moment I wasn't a part of it.

Things between my parents took a turn. As the fall set in, and the seasons changed, there was also, a change brewing within my mother. Not long after I was born, she finally had enough and separated from my father and was left to raise four children on her own, doing the best she could to provide and care for us.

Chapter Two
Trauma Conception

Trauma Conception is when two people of the opposite sex come together and conceive a child in an unhealthy condition. A man should refrain from alcohol or any drugs at least six months prior to impregnating a woman, and he should be supportive and gentle to her. A woman should cleanse her vessel of anything that is not good for her mental and emotional well-being. She should also be eating the right foods and getting proper rest!

They should be gentle to one another to create a healthy environment for the making of a God. Yes, a healthy child. Everything that the parents are dealing with during the time of conception is transferred to the embryo.

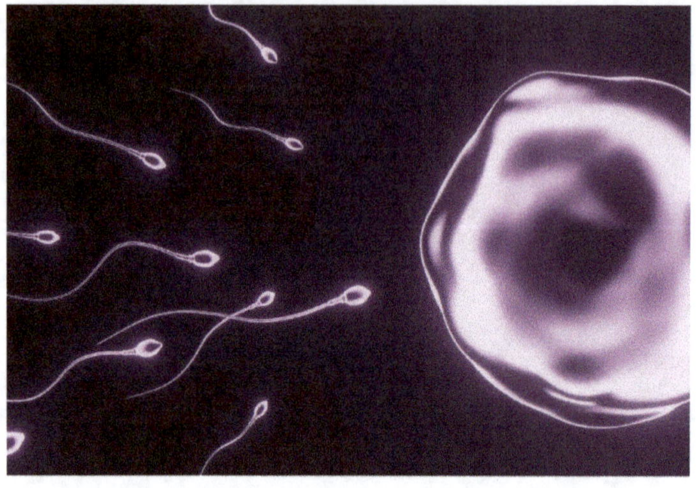

Trauma, depression, drugs, alcohol, stress, and anger etc. can be passed down. I carried on the depression. My mother was depressed when she conceived and as she carried me in her womb. As a young adult and in my adult years I made a lot of unwise decisions like having children at a young age, not completing high school, and leaving home early.

A lot of those decisions were made in those mentally unstable but functional times in my life. I also conceived and bore my children in the same way and in the same environment. Looking at my children seeing the reflection of me, and their father was so painful, and I felt helpless. I'm sorry that I introduced them to that kind of dysfunction but thank God we eventually found our way through our experiences.

Getting to the root cause of the things you are currently dealing with or have dealt with starts with asking your parents some questions. What was going on with them at the time of your conception? What trauma were they dealing with? How did they feel about each other? What was their mental, physical, emotional, and spiritual condition? It may also be beneficial to go deeper into the history of the generations that came before your parents. Learning more about yourself will help you understand your struggles and or the ways you view certain things in life.

Chapter Three
Birthing Position

When you are born, why is the correct position crown first? Why is that? The heart develops first. The first sign of life on a Sonogram is the electric current we see from the heart beating. The first thing we hear is the heartbeat. We don't see the brain beat or we can't hear the brain, but we can see and hear the heart.

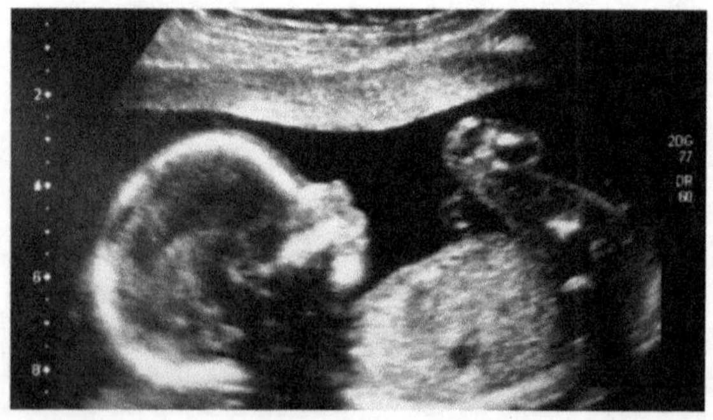

The crown, which houses the brain, is the first to come out of the womb. If born the original way. So, does the mind follow the heart? The heart is the first sign of life activity. Why do we not trust it? Why does the heart ask the mind questions?

The heart is the seat of our emotions and is viewed as the place of power. It is why we touch each other on an emotional level. If misused, it can turn into wanting power over others or operating from our envy or fear of our own energetic body. When I think of how we are born crown first, I can't help but wonder about the crown Chakra Energy Center known as the seat of wisdom. I will go into more detail about your Energy Centers in Chapter Thirteen.

Your heart and your mind send signals to each other. They question each other. The heart always refers to the mind for clarity, but the mind can sometimes be confused. The mind, the brain, the pineal gland which is the seat of the soul are all connected. What the mind sees and hears can cause internal conflict, when you're trying to choose which one to use or to believe. If you believe what you hear but see differently, which one are you going to believe? Many of us are by sight only people and then there are some of us who are driven by what we hear. Learning your-self will be very helpful for your journey, to use wisdom on when you must follow your heart and when you must listen to your mind.

To know others is wise but to know yourself is enlightenment!

Part II

Healing the Inside of You

Chapter Four
The Drug Called "Love"

We abuse our minds, bodies and souls with a drug called love. Love is an emotion, not something you can physically see. It's already in you, and it can be activated unknowingly.

It's a happy drug and it releases a chemical called serotonin which is secreted from the pineal gland. It's called the feel-good hormone which could affect your mood. You will start to chase it once you taste it. You may even forget to love yourself. You can become selfish and selfless at the same time, rebellious and resentful. These are the negatives and opposites of love, but they may be developed from disappointments of love failure.

Did you know that some people experience love withdraws? Yes, literally go through the motion of having to get it out of there system, if that means crying, depression, running away, chasing, turning to substances even sometimes killing! Is that what we call being "lovesick"?

I remember thinking about how grateful I was that I was never addicted to crack, alcohol, weed or pills, not realizing that I was addicted to love. Let me tell you, this thing called love it's just as bad as any of those drugs. By now you're probably laughing but it's true and some of y'all know what I'm talking about! And if not, good!

I'm sure by now, if you've ever been "lovesick" or addicted to love, you may be aware that you need a love doctor, a spiritual IV and heart paddles to restart the heart. A deep spiritual and love resuscitation.

Whatever you learn from love, use it as a benefit during your healing journey.

Chapter Five
Fixing Ourselves
Through Others

Do you suffer from the "If I fix them, I fix me" syndrome? The brokenness you see in them is often a reflection of the brokenness you have within. Your brokenness is attracted to fixing others. What you're giving away is what you need. You continuously give until you're depleted and because no one gives back to you, your box remains empty which only causes further damage.

Now, you're realizing you don't have a supplier for your needs. You're walking around unfilled without a sense of direction, just hoping one day someone would pour into your box. Healthy giving requires you to give from a full box and to surround yourself with others who give just as much as you do. Have you ever felt so passionately about helping someone who is out of control or broken? You feel so empathetic that it consumes you, your desire to fix them is your own brokenness. You may find yourself in broken moments with others because they are often mirrors reflecting to you the areas within that need healing. Fixing ourselves through others is a hidden gem but a painful journey.

One day I came across a passage in a book I was reading, and it was talking about how the airplane often goes against the wind while flying and when the plane encounters air pockets that cause turbulence, it straightens its wings to complete the assignment. The pilot controls the functions of the plane to make sure the mission is fulfilled. I thought about myself being that pilot and having control of the things I have allowed to attach themselves to my life., how storms and turbulence may come and shake your life up, but you have the ability to "straighten" your wings and bring yourself down the runway.

I want you to take a moment here to reflect. Ask yourself who have you tried to fix but ended up fixing yourself? Look at how it has brought you to a point where you had no choice but to patch up what you've broke within yourself trying to fix them. It's all a part of the lesson.

Chapter Six
Pained Bodies

You've heard the saying "hurt people hurt people" right? Pain trapped in the body are those things that hurt us that we have not yet released. Holding on to what has happened to you and reliving it as if it has happened again and again, keeps the pain within the body. Some pain is buried so deep that we suppress it until an event happens or a day comes that triggers the memory of that pain.

Certain smells or music can bring back a painful event or memory where it feels like it happened yesterday. Some pained bodies search for things like alcohol, drugs and or the comfort of a companion to take the pain away. I was attracted to other pained bodies, and they were attracted to me as well. I can't help but to believe I somehow felt a sense of familiarity. What I have learned by spending time with like-minded people is that we're all looking for something from each other to help grow pass the pain.

When I would have conversations with new friends, I learned we had similar past experiences, and we found comfort in sharing stories that we would normally keep inside. There were a lot of commonalities amongst us from choosing broken partners and that's just the surface of it all.

Releasing pain from the body may feel just as painful as receiving it because now you must release what's been buried, set it free, forgive and understand who you are today!

Pained bodies Practices that helped me was:
1. Acknowledging that there is pain there.
2. Bringing the pain that's in the body onto paper. Write it down no matter how much it is, get it onto paper. Once you've got it onto paper you may experience an overwhelming amount of feelings coming to the surface but this is the goal to get it out so that you can give it a proper disposal! After you feel a sense of relief you want to forgive whoever has caused you pain and if it was you, forgive yourself!
3. Say goodbye to the pain! Say "I release you, now you are no longer needed in my body. I've carried you long enough and now I let you go." Shred, burn or destroy the paper however you would like.

4. Now that you have released the pain you can move on! The memories will still be there if you decide to visit them, but the pain should have less and less control within the body as you continue healing.

Chapter Seven
Coming Undone

When coming undone, you must face reality. No more placing the blame on others or looking at external ways to label it. It's all yours now and how you decide to build it. Now, we're talking about you and your selfishness, your rebellion, your greed, your deception, and your conniving mind games. Using those things to get what you were needing or trying to get from others to compensate for your inadequacy and hidden pain. I'm talking about looking at yourself. It's easy to look at others and see their shortcomings but looking at yourself and how you've arrived at this point in your life, is where the real healing begins. When it's time to come undone, you're going to have to deal with you. Now, I'm not talking about the things that were out of your control like childhood molestation, rape, or things of that nature. I'm talking about things that were in your control, like sacrificing your identity to fit in or belong.

I remember the moment I realized I was selfish, and I am the most giving person I know and knew but honey, that was the problem. I didn't want to lose what I've gained so I kept giving from an empty box. I continued to hurt myself because I believed the more, I gave of me, the more I would have of you. Deposit after deposit until I realized that I was self-centered to the point it was toxic because I was only giving to receive something in return. Don't get me wrong, being self-centered is good if it's healthy and not being used to gain from others.

I realized there were some things I needed to give up and I needed to reflect upon what I had done and why I was adding to these already chaotic patterns. I had to scream with severe tears rolling down my eyes and a deep roar that came from my belly like I was finally purging myself. One day, one memory, one symptom at a time, which can take years to come undone. It's time to dig up and teardown and acknowledge what you've assisted with. Your desires and everything you thought even if you thought your way, was the best way.

It's time for you to travel a different road. You're going to have to leave behind some things, folks, and beliefs. Before you arrive at your next destination be sure your spiritual vehicle is well maintained. You must check out your engine, your wiring, your gas, your brakes. You may need a spiritual tune up to service your soul. Once you've done the work to your spiritual vehicle it is now ready for the road ahead. You are healing and coming undone

Chapter Eight
Carrying Your Cross

We are raised by our parents, no matter what kind of parent, no matter who your guardian is, you will be raised and guided by their decisions. Your environment, your food, your clothes, your education, and spirituality, it's your given identity as you prepare to grow while on earth. Your hard drive within you downloads all the information you accumulate daily. Some things you will use later and some things you may remember and there are somethings you may forget but nonetheless the information will help you along the way to get to your destination.

Carrying your cross is everything you have picked up along the way and not all of it is yours, but somehow it attached itself to you and you carried it. The Cross is heavy. Eventually you will leave the nesting of your parents. Your journey alone begins. You are now the adult, everything you accumulated from birth will continue to make your path good or bad. You are learning and unlearning. The choices you make now will more than likely be a result of your experiences so far.

The environment you grew up in plays a huge role in your decision making. While some people may choose to become a product of their environment there are others who choose to take a different path. Your Cross consists of all the love, pain, disappointment, your past, your family, your debt, your material gains, your losses, your job and much more. Some of things you have picked up along the way you will one day be ready to lay them down. Give them up and lighten your load.

Even the body is the shape of the cross, I believe it is symbolical for carrying your burdens. I was brought up in the church where they always stressed that Jesus already bore our sins and that all our sins are already forgiven, as I got older and realized that all the sins and mistakes I made, I paid for them. I couldn't understand, if they were already paid for then why am I dealing with the consequences of my actions? Well, now I know that Jesus was showing us the way and showing us how evil the world can be and how to endure and trust the journey of knowing self, seeking wisdom, while carrying our Cross.

Chapter Nine
Planted Seeds

Everything that grows has started with a seed. For seeds to grow into tangible things it must be planted in soil. When a farmer starts his or her garden, he has to make sure the soil is prepared to handle the growth of the seed.

One day I purchased a bag of beautiful pears. The color of the pear was nice, and the pear was soft and ready to be eaten. I couldn't wait to get home to wash the pears so I can consume it. After washing the pear, I took a bite into the pear and decided to look at the core and oh my God did I hurry up and spit it out. The core of the pear was rotten, I began to panic because I've already swallowed some of the rotten part. I was devastated to say the least and then I heard a soft voice inside saying to me "Everything that looks good ain't good. It's only what the physical eye can see and judge that makes you want to taste it." The temptation!

After that incident, I began to pay more attention to the seeds we cannot see and the soil in which they are planted, not all seeds are visible some seeds are thoughts and spoken words. Human bodies are the soil, and the information, thoughts and words are the seeds. Some humans are walking around every day living with either bad seeds or good seeds. You wouldn't know until you "bite" into them. Through observation and paying close attention to their conversations, their actions, their self-love or hate, you will begin to determine what type of seeds they are walking around carrying. You need to understand the seeds that were planted in you. What is the content of your conversations, what behaviors do you display in your relationships, do you practice self-love/ Listen to yourself when addressing others. Pay close attention to the seeds you are planting in your children, spouse, significant other, friends, family etc. The seeds that we plant will sure manifest one day into something tangible!

If there is something you are planning for the future, make sure you're preparing good soil and planting good seeds. Keep it a secret so that the only seeds that are growing in your garden is your thoughts and no one else's. How many times have you had a seed, and someone stole it or took your seed and manifested it before you did? Shh! just be silent and let it grow. Some of the best things are grown in the dark and quiet places without any disturbances! Plant good seeds within your mind, body and soul and in due time, you will see the manifestation of your harvest

Chapter Ten
Re-Wiring Process

Knowing the history and background of your building helps you rebuild yourself. I wanted to know more about me, so I went as far as understanding the condition of my conception. I wanted to understand deeper than just my experience. I needed to know my parent's experiences. My broken father lost his mother, my grandmother, at the tender age of two years old. Traumatically, someone took her away from him and my uncle. My grandfather would be the one to raise them, and of course, my great grandmother Patsy, may her soul rest in peace. Now, that I understand his trauma, I no longer blame him for what I didn't understand. He didn't provide mentally, or even physically but learning about him helped me to forgive him.

Rewiring things in a healthy way requires fixing the broken places. I had to come to an understanding within myself about the things that were out of my control regarding my father and letting go of the external blame. I began to rewire with better understanding and stopped searching for him in others.

My mother told me later in life that she stopped going to school at an early age and so did her mother. Man, did I blame her for so much of my inadequacy at one point in my life I judged what I thought I knew but when I would start to dig deep and ask her questions and hearing her answers, I saw her differently and realized she was the best mom anyone could ask for. She gave more than what she had I just didn't know it. My mother has a heart of gold and everything she has endured, she carried well. My new spark plug about her is built into my rewiring process.

The most challenging rewiring of them all, structured on my pain and confusion, and inadequacy was my relationships. Trauma met trauma and that was the catalyst for my deep thirst for happiness and healing. When you go through dark seasons in your relationships with your partner or friends, you have brought all your unhealed trauma into the connection. If both of you are dealing with unhealed trauma, it's a volcano waiting to erupt.

If it's one healed person joined with an unhealed person, it's just as bad because one person is suffering from the other person's unhealed issues struggling to understand the problems and missing links.

This brought me to a place where I needed to understand my partner's life. What I learned was that he was also broken, and the history of his birthing process was challenging as well.

Stripping myself down to nothing, desiring nothing and realizing that nothing is everything helped me start the rewiring process. Start with what you know now and what you've learned so far. Start rebuilding from there and keep going. Keep pushing past all the debris you have gotten rid of. Continue to see God's purpose and plan for your earthly life. Namaste.

Chapter Eleven
Keeping Your Candle Lit

There were ten virgins preparing for a particular event. This special event was the coming of the bridegroom who represents higher consciousness or Christ conscious as well as innocence and its inherent strength of endurance. It's also a lesson that we do not prepare for higher matters!

The ten virgins gathered their lamps and went forth to meet the bridegroom. Five of them were wise, and five were foolish. The virgins that were foolish took their lamps, but not enough oil but the wise virgins took oil in their vessels with their lamps and had extra oil.

As they set out on their journey the five foolish virgins ran out of oil and couldn't go on, they had to wait until morning to finish their journey. The other five virgins continued their journey because they had enough oil to see them through the night.

While the bridegroom tarried, they all slumbered and slept and at midnight there was a cry made, "Behold the bridegroom is coming, go out to meet him." The virgins rose and trimmed their lamps, and the foolish said unto the wise, "give us your oil for our lamps are gone out", but the wise assumed saying "not so, lest there be enough for us and you, but go ye to them that sell and buy yourselves some oil". While they went to buy oil, the bride groom came and those virgins that were ready went with him to the marriage, and the door was shut.

So many people are walking around with empty lamps or not enough oil in their lamps to keep going on this road of life here on earth. There are some people who do not know how to fill their lamps or prepare for upcoming events. They are often waiting hoping to glean from someone else's oil. Make sure you are walking around with enough, so when it's your time you're prepared. Your oil is your strength, your wisdom, your spiritual weapons.

We must be open to ourselves to endure the journey of a higher mind and emotions! What have you done to prepare your soul for the marriage? Check your oil!

Part III

Spiritual Practices for
The Soul

Chapter Twelve
Breathe

Most people are not aware that they are breathing shallow. Take a moment and pay attention to how you are breathing, you'll probably see that you're not taking breaths that goes deep into your lungs and belly. Sometimes your body will require you to take a deep breath and that breath will feel good to your body. Taking deep breaths is something to practice daily.

When I walk in my house and smell something I cooked yesterday I realize I need to open the windows so I can circulate the air within the house and remove the old stale air. I believe our bodies want that as well. Exchanging air is very great for our internal environment so remember to consciously breathe. The air that we breathe is shared with every living thing on earth and the universe, there's only one air but many bodies.

Practicing breathing is a great way to release stress and anxiety. Some ways you can practice breathing is by taking slow and steady inhales through your nose deep into your belly, then exhaling calmly and slow through your mouth, you can do this while driving, watching tv, taking a shower and so on! It would be great if you make this a daily practice and a part of your healing journey.

Chapter Thirteen
Energy Centers

We have energy centers in the body which all holds different functions. There are seven main centers that are lined up the spine to your crown. They are called chakras. There is a specific color associated with each chakra. Just like the rainbow, the chakra colors are in the same order.

The seventh chakra is located at the top of the head, which we call "the crown". The crown is associated with the color violet. The sixth chakra is located at the forehead which is also called the third eye chakra and is indigo and governs the brain. The fifth chakra is located at the throat and is blue and is associated with the element air. The fourth is at the heart, the thoracic region and gives life to the body. The third is located at the navel also called the solar plexus and is yellow and is associated with the fire element. The second is in the pelvic area and is orange and is symbolized by the water element. The first is located at the tail bone called the root chakra and is related to your connection to the earth.

Our energy centers are very vital to our life and to know them and their functions and how it pertains to your life will help bring enlightenment to you. Suffering is only learning and unlearning. When working on your energy centers its best to start with the lower chakras and work your way up to your higher chakras.

Working on the energy centers will improve your physical health. Its positive effects include stimulation of the metabolism, detoxification and strengthening of the immune system by infusing cells and organs with healing energy.

Here is one exercise I do that will help you practice connecting with your energy centers to aide you on your healing journey:

1. Find a place that you can use without interruptions
2. You can lie down or sit up
3. Close your eyes and take several deep breaths slowly inhaling deep and exhaling completely
4. Once relaxed, start with the first energy center, and work your way up to the seventh
5. Imagine the color associated with that energy, imagine each color getting brighter and moving in a circle. This will help move stagnant energy and your energy centers will start to balance

Chapter Fourteen
Meditation and Grounding

Meditation is important because it quiets the mind. Meditation allows you to see and hear pass the physical form. It allows you to become present in the moment. It's full of spiritual knowledge and enlightenment. It allows you to know God and the power within yourself. It's the stillness.

It's everything you need to know. It allows you to connect with who you truly are and takes you to a place of pure freedom.

Meditation allows you to see the temporary versus permanent. Inside the body is permanent spirit and soul. Outside of the body is temporary. All your illusions, anxieties, concerns, and issues are disappearing during meditation. We all need to take mental breaks away from the physical accumulation sometimes. Once you start to meditate and, it becomes a daily practice, you will see the difference it makes in your life.

In the previous chapter, I gave you an exercise you can practice, connecting with your energy centers. In this chapter, I'm going to share a similar practice that allows you to center yourself in the present moment. This is a meditation exercise I practice.

1. Find a quiet place without interruptions
2. You can lie down or sit up
3. Close your eyes and take several deep breaths slowly inhaling deep and exhaling completely
4. Your mind is going to try to continue it's mental chatter, but your goal is to tune out the noise of the mind
5. Keep taking deep breaths, relaxing your body as much as possible

6. Repeat each breath until your mind is calm

7. Keep your eyes close and you will begin to clear your conscious, this is the place of peace, the place of healing, I call this place nowhere but everywhere

As you practice this it gets easier each time you will also learn that this is where self-mastery of all things begins!

Next, I want to teach you about grounding. Grounding is recharging the body's energy. The earth is an energy supplier and to do grounding you must remove anything that would interrupt the connection(shoes). You can also lay on the ground and release any unwanted energies and at the same time receive energy from the earth.

Grounding is a wonderful stress reliever; our bodies are made of materials that are a part of

the earth. We share common elements, oxygen, calcium, sulfur, and magnesium.

Grounding reduces inflammation, pain, stress, improves blood flow, energy, and sleep. It's also an effective way to calm anxiety during a panic attack and generates greater well-being. Just like the trees are planted and stable and go through many storms being grounded and rooted is an important part of our life!

Whenever I've felt overwhelmed and needed to release unwanted feelings, I have found a space on the ground and laid there, and I have felt the unwanted energies leave my body and the strength of the earth enter! I literally got up feeling much better than I did before I laid down.

Chapter Fifteen
Natural Healers

The sun is not only for vitamin D, but it's also a natural healer. Yes, a healer. The heat that radiates from the sun heals. It is energy, which the body needs to keep moving. The sun is billions of miles away from the earth, yet it often feels as if there are no miles between us.

The sun circles around the earth in 30 days, then it starts a new journey, which become months and then years. Our bodies go through those cycles also because we're on an ever-moving Earth. A woman's menstrual cycle is identical to both the moon and the sun's cycles, and it sheds and starts every 28-30 days. We are blessed to experience the seasons change! When the seasons change externally, they also change internally. It's called different moods! You can experience spring, summer, winter and fall within, just know that the seasons change. Learning to identify your different seasons internally and being able to understand that it is a temporary change can help you get through the moments.

Some of us suffer with seasonal depression. I often notice this change during the fall season and I'm not feeling as jolly. I believe our bodies respond to the seasons as they come, although I love the fall, I seem to hate that the winter is approaching, and I cannot embrace it! So much comes with winter, living in the northern part of the world! Sometimes just doing certain things that comfort you, like candle lighting, nature walking, warm baths, eating your favorite foods, and swimming, etc. are all coping mechanisms to help us navigate the changing seasons.

We are here to learn lessons and elevate internally and our external environment is what helps us get there, not taking things personal but taking them as part of your lesson helps you get past the storms gracefully.

Water is also a natural healer; without it the world couldn't function! Water makes up sixty percent of the human body, seventy one percent of the earth is water. Water is also formed in the clouds and is used to water the earth. Water is a miracle; we need it, the power of it and the access we have to it, we should not take it for granted.

Drinking water has amazing benefits for our skin, heart, and kidneys. I am always amazed at how we can heal ourselves by connecting to the sun, the moon and water.

Chapter Sixteen
Nutrition

There are times, we go into phases where we forget about the care of our bodies. I have never wanted to carry excess weight but found myself getting thicker by the slice. I didn't realize that my mind played a huge role in maintaining a healthy weight. When your mind is cluttered and unhealthy trying to eat correctly is a lot of work and thought. I realized on my healing journey that nutrition has a lot to do with my mental health. Taking the holistic way, changing your diet, and eating the right foods will help your whole body get healthy. It's work, but with healing the mind, the body will follow.

Knowing your blood type will help you with a lot of the information about you. There's a blood type diet online that helps you learn about the foods that are not good for your blood type, and they also give you great examples of what foods are great to eat.

Giving the body, a break from solid food sometimes helps with the process of food being able to breakdown in the digestive system without overpowering it. The flow of nutrition is important for our body's proper function. Many diseases start in the stomach, undigested foods, and medication. The lining of the stomach is thin and must be healthy to break food down properly. Giving it a break, will help it detox. We have good and bad bacteria in the gut and acid. The Gut is our deciding station. It sends everything that enters to its proper place.

Become more conscious of your belly. For the medicine to work, it must be accepted properly into your system, some medicine will get into your body and your body does not accept it, the term for that is an allergic reaction. If your body does accept the medication it must go through several organs for it to work on the problem.

One area I find interesting is the brain once arriving to the brain, the brain's function adjusts to accommodate the medicine, so depending on the class of the medicine, it must sort out how it's going to work. One function is the pineal gland it's a gland in the brain that is the size of a grain of rice, but it's the most powerful gland in the body. It's the seat of all wisdom. The pineal gland is also shaped like the pinecone.

I became ill in 2019 due to overwhelming stress. My thyroid functions were in critical need of help. I found out that my pineal gland was full of hormones and couldn't release them. They had nowhere else to go, my thyroid gland was not functioning properly anymore. My T3 were sending hormones to my T4 which was just building up to the point It was too full to receive any more hormones so my T3 stopped sending anything because T4 wasn't accepting anymore.

Meanwhile, with it being off like that, it affected my organs, and my mind was clouded a lot. To get things back functioning properly, I was prescribed thyroid medicine, which had to tell the T3 to not send any hormones until the T4 is empty enough to accept more of the hormone. All of this may have been prevented if the stress was under control and my nutrition was better. Today I am medication free. I am grateful it took three years of determination, healthy nutrition, working out and less stress. You are truly what you eat.

Chapter Seventeen
Balance

Feminine and masculine energy. At conception, your genes will later form to determine your sex. In the beginning you are neither. As a child, I chose to use more of my masculine gene, maybe because of my experience in my mother's womb I may have felt her struggle and fought to survive the journey. It's possible I was surely off balanced. You couldn't force me into a dress, and I was a tough little girl. My aunt once said to me when I became a teenager that she didn't think I'll turn out as cute as I did. I would carry this masculine energy into my young adulthood relationships, which grew even stronger as I found myself using more of my masculine energy.

The way I carried myself was very strong, yet soft. Finding a balance was hard for me because I had to live through it to learn balance. There are two sides to everything. The body has two sides and on the body there's two of everything. Two eyes, two eyebrows, two lips, two nostril holes. Each tooth has a twin, two guns, two ears, but two different sides make up one body.

The tongue is one but holds the most power. It gives you the power to speak, but it also has two sides and if you look underneath the tongue, it has a ligament in the middle that shows it has two sides. The tongue is responsible for taste. Therefore, words that come from the mouth, the tongue has the power to taste it before it spits it out. Words, good or bad, must come through the tongue to leave the body. The mind creates the words because it starts with a thought. The thought then travels to the throat, which is responsible for sound, the vibrations of sound send signals to the mouth to open where the tongue must move for the words to come out and come to life. What you speak goes out into the universe where others can now hear and receive from you.

When it comes to balance, there's a good and bad side to everything. In the world there's dark and light. The balance symbol teaches us that. It's one whole circle representing one body with two sides. One side is dark, the other side is light. Each side holds its own energy. Even the sun reflects its light on the moon so it can shine, one represents day and the other night. Everything happens for a reason. It is a part of the cycle, whether it's good or bad.

The universe is living in every human being and is living according to its flow. We are a mass of humans with the same flow as the universe. Uni, meaning one, verse meaning flow. We are Uni with verse but several bodies, we are everywhere. In the Bible, God says "I am everywhere" I see and know all! Omnipresent, God is everywhere. You are the sun. You are the stars. You are everything that consists of the universe. Finding the balance and healing the inside of you will allow you to transcend consciously as you journey though this life.

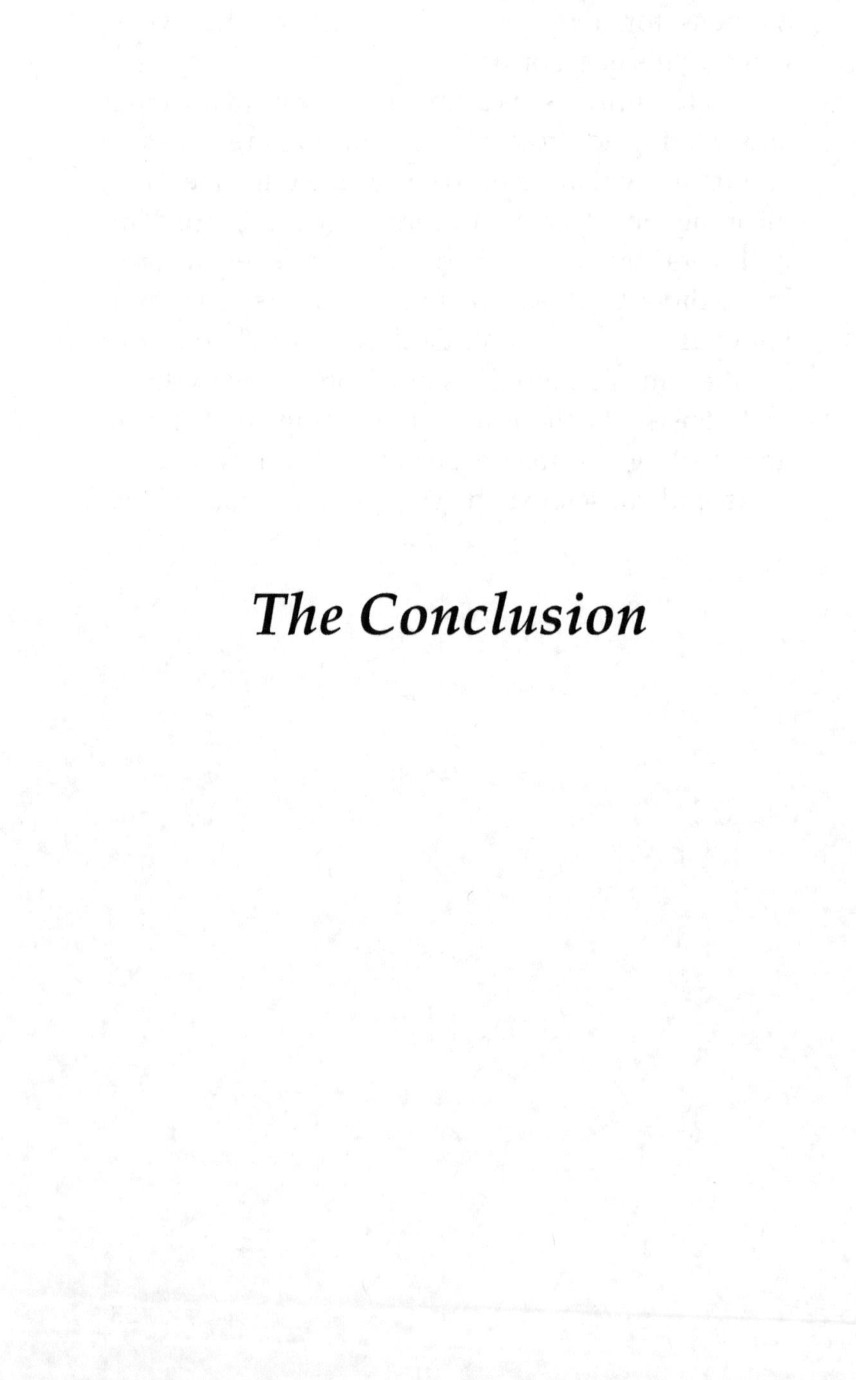

The Conclusion

Conclusion

My hope was to put multiple subjects together for you in one place that helped me along the way on my healing journey. I pray this book finds you at a time that you need it. I hope my experiences will be a light to someone else! I believe my purpose is to help others that's hurting find their way to healing! My soul rejoices when I see people become healed holistically mind, body, and soul by discovering their life path! What we call pain can be a gain if we understand what it has taught us.

I also wanted to gift you with a few journal pages in the back of the book, as an aide to assist you in your healing. Namaste'

Journal

THE INSIDE OF YOU

THE INSIDE OF YOU

THE INSIDE OF YOU

THE INSIDE OF YOU

THE INSIDE OF YOU

THE INSIDE OF YOU